KS2 Success SATs

Level 3

English

LEARN AND PRACTISE

Alison Head

Contents

Speaking and listening

Speaking and listening skills 4

Reading

The language of books 6
Fiction and non-fiction 8
Reading skills 10
Authors and narrators 12
Life stories 14

Writing

Sentences 16
Contractions 18
Possessive apostrophes 20
Punctuation 22
Writing about speech 24
Nouns and pronouns 26
Plurals 28
Adjectives 30
Verbs 32
Adverbs 34
Synonyms 36
Imagery 38
Special effects 40
Instructions 42
Persuasive writing 44
Recounts 46
Reports 48
Planning stories 50
Characters and settings 52
Poetry 54

Glossary

Glossary 56

Answers

Answer booklet (detach from centre of book) 1–4

Speaking and listening skills

Taking turns

The **speaking and listening** skills you learn at school will help you to speak clearly to an audience and also to understand what other people are saying to you.

You might be asked to give your own presentation, or to listen to a presentation on a topic. Or you might be asked to discuss a topic with another person, or in a group. Very often, you will have to wait for your turn to speak.

When someone is speaking, it is polite to stay quiet. It also means you can listen carefully to what they say. You might even want to make some quick notes to remind you of the key points they make.

Getting ready to speak

Speaking in front of a group can be scary, but being properly prepared will make you more confident.

Start by gathering the information you need. You might need to do some research in books or on the Internet. If you are working in a team, discuss your ideas with the others in your team.

Make notes of your ideas and decide which are the most important. You should talk about these first.

 Top Tip Try to learn the main points you want to make, using your notes to help you.

 Key words   speaking and listening

Taking turns

Working with a partner, discuss what you did over the summer holiday. Remember to take turns.

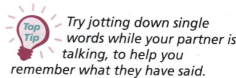 *Try jotting down single words while your partner is talking, to help you remember what they have said.*

Write down two of the points you make about your holiday.

1 _____

2 _____

Write down two of the points your partner makes.

3 _____

4 _____

4

Getting ready to speak

Imagine you are planning a short presentation on one of your hobbies. Write down **four** key points you would like to make.

1 _____

2 _____

3 _____

4 _____

4

TOTAL MARKS   8

The language of books

On the cover

The first thing you see when you look at a book is the front cover. A lot of the features you find on the cover of a book are designed to encourage people to pick up the book and read it. Others are there to help bookshops and libraries.

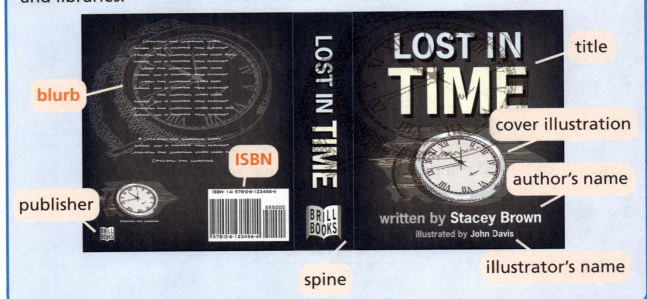

Inside books

The insides of books are designed to make reading them easier. Information books arrange their contents so that it is easy for readers to find what they need.

The contents list is at the front of the book. It lists the chapters or sections in the book, along with the page each starts on. Contents lists are arranged in page order.

The **index** is found at the back of the book. Indexes list subjects alphabetically, to help readers find information about a specific topic.

Information books often contain new words. Some books explain what these words mean. Often they are listed alphabetically at the back of the book, along with their definitions. This is called a **glossary**.

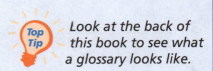 *Look at the back of this book to see what a glossary looks like.*

 Key words   **blurb**   **ISBN**   **index**   **glossary**

On the cover

Think about your favourite book, or the book you are reading now. Design a new front cover for it. You will score one mark for including each of the following three things:
a title, a cover illustration and the name of the author.

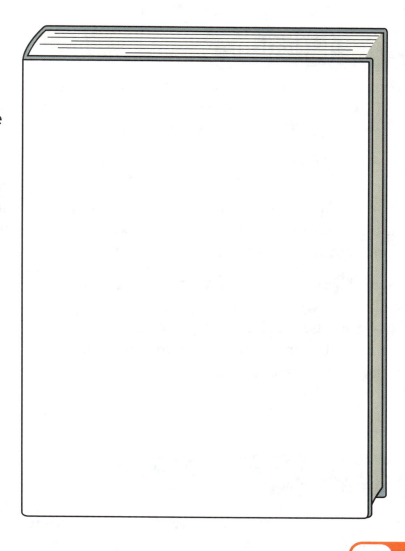

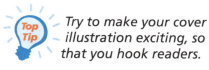 *Try to make your cover illustration exciting, so that you hook readers.*

3

Inside books

Choose the correct option to complete each sentence. Underline your choice.

1   The contents list is found at the (back / front) of the book.

2   The index is arranged (alphabetically / in page order).

3   New words are explained in a (blurb / glossary).

4   There is a glossary at the (back / front) of this book.

5   The index is found at the (front / back) of the book.

5

TOTAL MARKS 8

Fiction and non-fiction

What is fiction?

Fiction is made-up writing. Most of the short stories and longer novels you read are fiction. They contain made-up characters and settings, and the events that happen are made up too.

Some fiction writing is based on a real person, or set in a real place. Other stories might be about real things that happened. However, most of the details come from the writer's imagination.

Fiction writing is designed to be read right the way through, so you can follow the story. Good fiction is so gripping that you don't want to put it down until you know what happens at the end!

What is non-fiction?

Non-fiction is information writing. Books about science, history or animals are all non-fiction and so are newspapers, adverts and instructions. This book is non-fiction too!

Non-fiction writing contains lots of **facts**. The information is usually organised into chapters or sections, so that readers can find what they need easily, rather than having to read the whole book.

Top Tip: You need to know the difference between fiction and non-fiction. It can be hard to tell sometimes, because writers often base fictional stories on real people or events.

 Key words   fiction   non-fiction   fact

What is fiction?

Look at this pile of books. Can you tell by their titles which ones are fiction? Colour the fiction books red and the non-fiction books blue.

Top Tip: Non-fiction books often have straightforward titles that tell you exactly what is inside the book.

5

What is non-fiction?

Do you enjoy non-fiction books? Or do you prefer fiction?

1 _____

_____

Write a sentence to explain why you think this is.

2 _____

_____

2

TOTAL MARKS 7

Reading skills

Skimming

Reading tests ask questions to check **comprehension**, or understanding, of a piece of writing. We read in different ways, depending on what we are trying to find out from a piece of writing.

When you see a piece of writing for the first time, you will often read through it quickly, to find out what it is about. You might also notice how it is organised. If it is fiction, perhaps you will notice where the characters first appear and what they are like. If it is non-fiction, you will be able to work out what kind of writing it is and spot where the topic changes.

Quick reading for meaning like this is called **skimming**.

Scanning

Once you have skimmed through the text and read the questions carefully, you are ready to look for the information you need to answer them.

Scanning means reading the text again, looking for a specific piece of information. It might be a person's name, a date or the name of a place. The way the question is worded will tell you what kind of information you need to look for.

Where did the family in the story move to?	Look for a place name.
When did Henry VIII come to the throne?	Look for a date.

 Take care with scanning. There may be more than one place name or date in the text and you won't get any marks if you choose the wrong one!

 Key words   comprehension   skimming   scanning

10

Skimming

Skim through this piece of text, then answer the questions.

For a week now, piles of clean, ironed laundry had been growing in the bedrooms of the Clarks' house. Milly's mum was working hard to get the family ready for their trip to Florida.

Like all ten-year-olds, Milly loved to try new things and swimming with the dolphins on this trip was all she thought about. That, and her dog Max, who would be going into kennels for the first time. She would miss him!

1 What is the piece of writing about? Circle your answer.

   a family holiday   a kennel   laundry

2 Is the story about a girl or a boy?

   _____

3 Do you think it is fiction or non-fiction?

   _____

Scanning

Use your scanning skills to find the answers to these questions.

1 How old is Milly?   _____

2 What is her dog called?   _____

3 Where is the family going on holiday?   _____

Authors and narrators

What is an author?

Someone who writes a piece of text is called an **author**.

Most fiction books only have one author, who writes the whole story. A fiction book is a story that comes from the imagination of the author.

Some non-fiction books have more than one author. This can happen where the book contains information about more than one topic and each author writes about the topic they know best. Other times, two authors will work together to research and write a non-fiction book about a single topic.

It is important to know the name of a book's author, because bookshops and libraries arrange books alphabetically, by author.

What is a narrator?

The **narrator** is the storyteller in a piece of fiction writing. Narrators tell the story from their point of view. Sometimes the narrator is the author. Remember that this type of narrator can see all of the **characters** all of the time and knows exactly how they are all feeling. Clever!

> The boy ran across the park and headed towards the station.

Other times, the narrator is a character in the story. This type of narrator will tell the story through the eyes of the character.

> I ran across the park and headed for the station.

Top Tip: Non-fiction books don't have a narrator, because they don't tell a story. They are written in an impersonal way, to describe and explain the topic.

 Key words   author   narrator   character

What is an author?

Answer these questions about authors.

1 What is an author?

   _____

   _____

2 If a book has more than one author, is it more likely to be fiction or non-fiction?

   _____

3 How do libraries and bookshops use the names of authors?

   _____

   _____

What is a narrator?

Answer these questions about narrators.

1 Write a sentence to explain what a narrator is.

   _____

   _____

2 In this piece of text, is the narrator a character in the story?

   > Hearing steps in the hallway outside, I slipped behind the curtain, tucking my feet out of sight.

   yes ☐   no ☐

   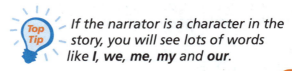 *If the narrator is a character in the story, you will see lots of words like **I**, **we**, **me**, **my** and **our**.*

Life stories

Biography

A **biography** is the story of a person's life, written by someone else.

Quite often, biographies are about people from history. Writers do lots of research to find out about their lives.

> Her family moved to Somerset during the war. She and her brother started at the local school. At first the other children treated them with suspicion, but when the evacuees arrived from London it was easier to fit in.

Autobiography

Autobiographies are life stories too, but they are written by the person whose story they tell.

> My family moved to Somerset during the war. My brother and I started at the local school. At first the other children treated us with suspicion, but when the evacuees arrived from London it was easier to fit in.

Top Tip: A **curriculum vitae**, or CV, is another type of life story. People write a CV when they are looking for a new job, to show their qualifications and experience.

Key words: biography   autobiography   curriculum vitae

14

Biography

Can you tell biography from autobiography? Decide whether each of these sentences is more likely to have come from a biography or an autobiography. Write B for biography, or A for autobiography, in the boxes.

1 He produced the first maps of New Zealand. ☐

2 Our house had a small yard at the back, with an outside toilet. ☐

3 Her dress designs are seen on catwalks across the globe. ☐

4 I have always wanted to swim with dolphins. ☐

5 My childhood dream came true when I made it into the Olympic team. ☐

 *The writers of autobiography are writing about their own lives, so they will use words like **I**, **me**, **my** and **our**.*

5

Autobiography

Imagine you are writing your autobiography. You will get one mark each for writing about where you were born, where you live now, your family, friends and school.

_____

_____

_____

_____

_____

_____

5

TOTAL MARKS 10

Sentences

Rules for sentences

A sentence is a group of words that work together to make sense on their own. They allow us to say what we think, ask questions and tell people what to do.

When we write sentences, there are some rules that we have to follow. The first word in a sentence must always start with a capital letter. This helps readers to understand that a new sentence has started.

Most sentences end with a full stop, but questions end with a question mark instead. If the sentence is delivering a surprise, or an order, it ends with an exclamation mark.

Is it time for dinner yet?

Look, it's snowing!

Clauses

A clause is part of a sentence that contains both a verb and a subject. A subject is the person or thing doing the action.

Some sentences just contain one clause. They are called simple sentences.

Ben ate the banana.

subject   verb

Some sentences contain more than one clause.

Ben ate the banana because he was hungry.

clause 1   clause 2

Often clauses in sentences are linked with joining words, like **because** in the example above.

Top Tip: Clauses do not have capital letters or full stops, unless they form a simple sentence.

 Key words sentence   question mark   exclamation mark   clause
verb   subject   simple sentence

16

Rules for sentences

Can you find a mistake in each of these sentences? Circle them when you find them.

1 Stop that dreadful noise.

2 Where is my coat.

3 The bus was late, so we missed the start of the film

4 we are going to France on holiday.

5 it was my birthday on Friday.

5

Clauses

Decide which of these statements about clauses are true or false.

1 Simple sentences only contain one clause. _____

2 Sentences cannot contain more than one clause. _____

3 Clauses within sentences are often joined together with joining words. _____

4 Clauses do not contain a verb. _____

5 Clauses do not usually have a full stop or capital letter. _____

5

TOTAL MARKS 10

17

Contractions

How contractions work

Sometimes we use the same pairs of words so often that we can join them together. This is called contraction.

Words are contracted by removing one or more letters and replacing them with an apostrophe. Then you simply join the two words together.

I am = I'm   you will = you'll

I'm great at contractions and soon you'll be great too!

Top Tip We use contraction all the time when we write conversation, or dialogue, for our characters. It is not usually used in more formal writing, like school work.

Writing contracted forms

Here are some examples of contractions we use a lot.

she is	→	she's
does not	→	doesn't
he will	→	he'll
I have	→	I've
is not	→	isn't
who is	→	who's
you are	→	you're
they will	→	they'll
did not	→	didn't
they are	→	they're

I've got 10 sweets!

I haven't got any!

Key words   contraction   apostrophe   dialogue

How contractions work

Circle the correct contracted form for each pair of words.

1 he is   hei's   hes   he's
2 we will   well   we'll   we'l
3 she would   she'd   shew'd   she'ld
4 could not   couldnt   could't   couldn't
5 she will   she'll   she'l   shell

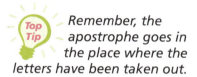
Top Tip: Remember, the apostrophe goes in the place where the letters have been taken out.

5

Writing contracted forms

Can you write down the contracted forms of these word pairs?

1 you will   _____
2 you have   _____
3 we are   _____
4 I would   _____
5 should not   _____

5

TOTAL MARKS   10

Possessive apostrophes

Using possessive apostrophes

Possessive apostrophes can be used to show that something belongs to someone or something.

You write them by adding an apostrophe followed by *s*.

> the book that belongs to Sam = Sam's book
>
> the basket that belongs to the dog = the dog's basket
>
> the rattle that belongs to the baby = the baby's rattle

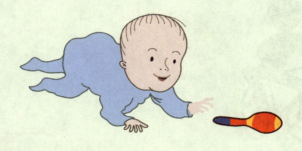

Possessive apostrophes for groups

Sometimes you will need to add a possessive apostrophe to a word that already ends in *s* because it is a **plural**.

In this case, you just add the apostrophe without adding another *s*.

> the cars that belong to the teachers = the teachers' cars
>
> the burrows that belong to the rabbits = the rabbits' burrows
>
> the bags that belong to the boys = the boys' bags

 It is important to put the apostrophe in the correct place, because it is one of the ways your reader can tell whether you are talking about one person, or more than one.

 Key words   possessive apostrophe   plural

20

Using possessive apostrophes

Add the possessive apostrophe to each sentence.

1 Dawns shoes were too small.

2 I found the dogs lead and took him for a walk.

3 My sisters room is bigger than mine.

4 Tims birthday is next Friday.

5 A ducks feathers keep it warm and dry.

Possessive apostrophes for groups

Choose the correct word from the brackets to complete each sentence and write it in.

1 Three _____ faces appeared at the window. (boy's / boys')

2 All of our school _____ houses are a bus ride away. (friend's / friends')

3 All four _____ windows were decorated with Christmas lights. (shops' / shop's)

4 The sound of many _____ engines filled the air. (car's / cars')

5 Our two _____ claws had left scratches on the furniture. (cats' / cat's)

Top Tip — When you are deciding where to put a possessive apostrophe, look at whether the sentence is talking about one person or thing, or more than one.

TOTAL MARKS 10

Punctuation

What is punctuation for?

We use **punctuation** to help our readers understand our writing. Punctuation marks work like a code to help readers to know when to pause, when someone is speaking and when a new topic is beginning. Without punctuation, reading would be much harder. Try reading this!

> marys feet slipped on the steep path and she lost her balance help she screamed her voice echoed around the canyon there was nobody to hear her she clung to the ledge and waited as the sun grew hotter

Ending sentences

Some of the most important punctuation marks end sentences. They tell readers that a sentence has finished and a new one is about to begin, and what kind of sentence it is.

Most sentences end with a full stop, but questions end with a question mark.

> I finished my book.   Have you seen Emily?

Sentences that deliver a surprise or an order end with an exclamation mark.

> Happy birthday!   Get out!

Commas

Commas are useful punctuation marks that help readers to make sense of sentences.

> Cackling loudly, the witch swept out of the cave.

Commas are also useful for separating the items in a list.

> We saw lions, tigers, giraffes and monkeys at the zoo.

Top Tip: Remember, you do not put a comma before the final **and** in a list.

 Key words   punctuation   comma

What is punctuation for?

Circle the punctuation marks in this piece of writing.

1. Greg ran down the stairs two at a time and bounded through the kitchen, grabbing a piece of toast on the way.

2. "Where are you off to?" asked Dad.

3. "I'm late for school!" panted Greg.

4. Dad laughed, "Greg, it's Saturday!"

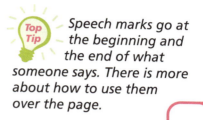

Top Tip Speech marks go at the beginning and the end of what someone says. There is more about how to use them over the page.

Ending sentences

Choose a full stop, question mark or exclamation mark to complete each sentence.

1. What time is it _____

2. We went to the theatre on Saturday _____

3. I don't believe it _____

4. How are you feeling _____

Commas

Add commas to these sentences.

1. I need to buy pencils a ruler and a sharpener for school.

2. Alex James Jack and Ali got parts in the school play.

3. I packed pyjamas slippers a toothbrush and toothpaste for the sleepover party.

4. We made a fruit smoothie with bananas strawberries raspberries and pears.

Writing about speech

Direct and reported speech

We often need to write about the things that people say.

Sometimes we write speech for our characters, so that they can talk to each other. We write the actual words that they say.

> "What would you like for tea?" asked Dad.

This is called **direct speech**.

Other times we can write what someone says, without using their exact words.

> Dad asked us what we wanted to eat.

This is called **reported speech**.

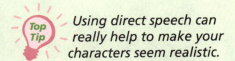

Top Tip: *Using direct speech can really help to make your characters seem realistic.*

Speech punctuation

When you write direct speech, you must use speech punctuation. It separates the speech from the rest of the sentence, so that your readers understand when someone is talking.

> The teacher shouted, "Stop it!"

Speech marks go at the beginning and end of the speech, in pairs. When somebody is speaking, remember that their words always start with a capital letter, even if they are not at the start of a sentence.

 Key words   **direct speech**   **reported speech**   **speech marks**

Direct and reported speech

Decide whether each sentence contains direct or reported speech. Write direct or reported at the end of each sentence.

1 "Have you seen my coat?" asked Sammy. _____

2 The shopkeeper told us the shop was about to close. _____

3 Christine complained, "It's very cold in here." _____

4 The teacher told the class to put their books away. _____

4

Speech punctuation

These sentences contain direct speech. Add the missing speech marks.

1 The librarian explained, "The fiction books are over there.

2 Where have you been?" asked Daniel.

3 Tim asked, "Why were you late?

4 "How much does that cost? asked Andrew.

4

TOTAL MARKS 8

Nouns and pronouns

Common nouns

Common nouns name ordinary things.

book   pen   cat

Common nouns do not start with a capital letter, unless they are at the beginning of a sentence.

The rabbit hopped away.   Rabbits hopped around us.

Proper nouns

Proper nouns name people, places and things like the days of the week and the months of the year.

London   March   Annabel

Proper nouns begin with a capital letter, wherever they appear in a sentence.

Pronouns

Pronouns can sometimes be used in place of a **noun**.

I, she, me, him, we, them

They can save you from having to keep using the same noun again and again.

I couldn't find **Sam**.   I couldn't find **him**.

 The pronoun I is always a capital letter.

 Key words   common noun   proper noun   pronoun   noun

Common nouns

Underline the common nouns in these sentences.

1. The cat was asleep.
2. Jonathon lost his bag.
3. Gran took an umbrella because it was raining.

[3]

Proper nouns

Circle the proper nouns in the box for one mark each.

Tuesday   box   house   Spain   guitar

Robert   wall   January   Friday   horse   fire

Cardiff   Worcester   desk   family   Barbara

[8]

Pronouns

Underline the pronoun in each sentence.

1. Mum asked George if he was hungry.
2. Jane and Kate ran for the bus, but they were too slow.
3. Luke stroked the cat, but it ran away.

[3]

TOTAL MARKS [14]

Plurals

What is a plural?

Plural means more than one of something.

books

toys

bananas

Nouns are the only type of words that have singular and plural forms.

Writing plurals

With many nouns, you can just add an *s* to make the plural.

flower	flowers
chair	chairs
bird	birds

If the word ends in *ss*, *x*, *zz*, *sh* or *ch*, you must add *es* to make the plural.

cross	crosses
box	boxes
bush	bushes
church	churches

Top Tip Try saying plurals out loud to help you to spell them. You can often hear the *e* in *es* plurals.

Key words singular plural

What is a plural?

1. Write down your own definition for the word *plural* for one mark.

   _____

2. Circle the plural words. You will get a mark for each one.

balls	dress	bush	schools
ink	bags	loss	wishes
eyes	table	mouse	horses

   7

Writing plurals

Write down the plurals of these words.

1. kiss   _____

2. fox   _____

3. pencil   _____

4. fence   _____

5. wish   _____

6. ditch   _____

7. dog   _____

8. star   _____

8

TOTAL MARKS   15

Adjectives

What is an adjective?

Adjectives are words that describe nouns. They can help you to describe what colour, shape or size something is.

The **car** was **red**.

noun   adjective

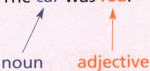

The lawn was **square**.

I ordered a **huge** ice cream.

Choosing adjectives

Adjectives will make your writing more interesting to read, because your readers will find it easier to imagine what you are describing.

Some adjectives work harder than others. Try to avoid using boring adjectives like *big*, *small* or *nice*. Try to think of more interesting alternatives that say more about the thing you are describing.

big	enormous	huge	massive
small	tiny	minute	petite
nice	kind	thoughtful	friendly

Top Tip: Look out for strong adjectives when you are reading. Make a note of ones you could use in your own writing.

Key words   adjective

Answers

PAGE 5
Taking turns
Answers will vary, but one mark should be awarded for each point noted.

Getting ready to speak
Answers will vary, but one mark should be awarded for each point noted.

PAGE 7
On the cover
Answers will vary, but one mark should be awarded for each of the following features on the cover: title, cover illustration, name of author.

Inside books
1 front
2 alphabetically
3 glossary
4 back
5 back

PAGE 9
What is fiction?
Fiction: The Christmas Pony, Nasty Nigel, Martin's Mountain
Non-fiction: Cricket, Scotland

What is non-fiction?
Answers will vary, but one mark should be given for stating a preference between fiction and non-fiction, and one mark for writing a sentence explaining the preference.

PAGE 11
Skimming
1 a family holiday
2 a girl
3 fiction

Scanning
1 10 years old
2 Max
3 Florida

PAGE 13
What is an author?
1 An author is a person who writes a text.
2 non-fiction
3 To arrange books alphabetically.

What is a narrator?
1 Sentences will vary, but might include: A narrator is the storyteller in a piece of fiction.
2 yes

PAGE 15
Biography
Biography: 1, 3
Autobiography: 2, 4, 5

Autobiography
Answers will vary, but one mark should be awarded for each of the following features: writer's birthplace, current home, family, friends and school.

PAGE 17
Rules for sentences
1 Stop that dreadful noise.
2 Where is my coat?
3 The bus was late, so we missed the start of the film.
4 We are going to France on holiday.
5 It was my birthday on Friday.

Clauses
True: 1, 3, 5
False: 2, 4

PAGE 19
How contractions work
1 he's
2 we'll
3 she'd
4 couldn't
5 she'll

Writing contracted forms
1 you'll
2 you've
3 we're
4 I'd
5 shouldn't

PAGE 21
Using possessive apostrophes
1 Dawn's shoes were too small.
2 I found the dog's lead and took him for a walk.

1

3 My sister's room is bigger than mine.
4 Tim's birthday is next Friday.
5 A duck's feathers keep it warm and dry.

Possessive apostrophes for groups
1 boys'
2 friends'
3 shops'
4 cars'
5 cats'

PAGE 23
What is punctuation for?
1 Greg ran down the stairs two at a time and bounded through the kitchen, grabbing a piece of toast on the way.
2 "Where are you off to?" asked Dad.
3 "I'm late for school!" panted Greg.
4 Dad laughed, "Greg, it's Saturday!"

Ending sentences
1 What time is it?
2 We went to the theatre on Saturday.
3 I don't believe it!
4 How are you feeling?

Commas
1 I need to buy pencils, a ruler and a sharpener for school.
2 Alex, James, Jack and Ali got parts in the school play.
3 I packed pyjamas, slippers, a toothbrush and toothpaste for the sleepover party.
4 We made a fruit smoothie with bananas, strawberries, raspberries and pears.

PAGE 25
Direct and reported speech
Direct speech: 1, 3
Reported speech: 2, 4

Speech punctuation
1 The librarian explained, "The fiction books are over there."
2 "Where have you been?" asked Daniel.
3 Tim asked, "Why were you late?"
4 "How much does that cost?" asked Andrew.

PAGE 27
Common nouns
1 The cat was asleep.
2 Jonathon lost his bag.
3 Gran took an umbrella because it was raining.

Proper nouns
The proper nouns are: Tuesday, Spain, Robert, January, Friday, Cardiff, Worcester, Barbara.

Pronouns
1 Mum asked George if he was hungry.
2 Jane and Kate ran for the bus, but they were too slow.
3 Luke stroked the cat, but it ran away.

PAGE 29
What is a plural?
1 Answers will vary, but might include: A plural means more than one of something.
2 The plurals are: balls, eyes, bags, schools, wishes, horses.

Writing plurals
1 kisses
2 foxes
3 pencils
4 fences
5 wishes
6 ditches
7 dogs
8 stars

PAGE 31
What is an adjective?
1 The Earth is round.
2 The cake was delicious.
3 Dad told us a funny joke.
4 Our teacher was happy because we finished our work.
5 The beautiful ballerina danced across the stage.

Choosing adjectives
Answers will vary, but might include:
1 A tiny spider had spun a web among the grass.
2 The naughty boy stuck out his tongue.
3 I am reading a brilliant book.

PAGE 33
Verbs are action words
1 The boy kicked the ball.
2 It rained all day.
3 The horse trotted around its field.
4 Our teacher collected the books.
5 The man hobbled down the street.

Using verbs
1 The girl ate the cake.
2 A bus takes us to school.
3 Our goldfish swims around its bowl.
4 I love helping Mum in the kitchen.
5 We planned a big party for Dad's birthday.

Verb tenses
1 We all (laughed) at Philip's joke.
2 The scouts (cooked) sausages on a campfire.
3 Our hamster (climbed) up the bars of its cage.
4 My class (collected) money for charity.
5 I (looked) for my missing football boot.

PAGE 35
How do adverbs work?
1 The plane climbed <u>steadily</u>.
2 Dad yawned <u>sleepily</u>.
3 The children waved <u>cheerfully</u>.
4 We crossed the road <u>carefully</u>.
5 Eve did her homework <u>neatly</u>.

Adverbs and verbs
1 The boy shouted angrily at his younger brother.
2 Amy read her story nervously to the class.
3 Connor ran quickly to answer the door.
4 The girls asked politely for a drink.
5 A bird swooped suddenly over the garden.

PAGE 37
What are synonyms?

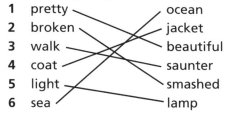

Using synonyms
Answers may vary, but might include:
1 The dark corridor led into a gloomy courtyard.
2 The cupboard held a dustpan and brush and a long-handled broom.
3 We walked across the field to a flowery meadow, where we ate our picnic.
4 I rushed out of the house and hurried to catch the bus.

PAGE 39
Simile
1 Tom gobbled up his pizza <u>like a pig</u>.
2 Katie answered the door <u>as fast as lightning</u>.

3 The laundry fluttered on the line <u>like bunting</u>.
4 The kitten's fur was <u>as soft as silk</u>.

Metaphor
Sentences 1 and 3 contain metaphors.

Personification
1 The moon smiled down on us.
2 The branches of the trees reached out into the darkness.
3 Shadows crept across the floor towards us.
4 A strong wind chased dry autumn leaves off the trees.

PAGE 41
Alliteration
1 Billy bounced a blue ball.
2 Paul paid Peter a pound.
3 Sarah saw silver stars sparkling.
4 Autumn leaves tumbled from towering treetops.
5 Whistling winds whipped wispy clouds.

Onomatopoeia

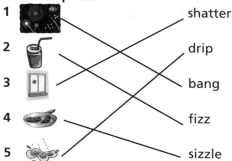

PAGE 43
What are instructions?
1 <u>Melt</u> the chocolate over a low heat.
2 <u>Add</u> the crisp rice cereal.
3 <u>Stir</u> until the cereal is coated with the melted chocolate.
4 <u>Spoon</u> the mixture into paper cake cases.
5 <u>Refrigerate</u> until set.

Writing instructions
1 Wet hair thoroughly.
2 Apply shampoo.
3 Work shampoo into a lather.
4 Rinse thoroughly.
5 Dry hair.

PAGE 45
Types of persuasive writing
The following are types of persuasive writing: a magazine advert, a poster advertising a film,

a leaflet about a new leisure centre, a holiday brochure.

The language of persuasion
1   Sentence b) is more persuasive.
2   Space Battles is an <u>exciting</u> film packed with <u>incredible</u> special effects and starring the <u>biggest</u> names in Hollywood.
3   Sentence b) has more powerful adjectives.

PAGE 47
What is a recount?
Answers will vary, but might include:
1   a biography
2   an account of a school trip
3   a story about something funny that happened

Writing a recount
We went to the animal rescue centre to adopt a pet cat. <u>First</u> we looked at some kittens and <u>then</u> an old black cat. <u>After that</u> we saw a lovely tabby with white paws, <u>followed</u> by a black fluffy cat. <u>Finally</u> we chose a beautiful tortoiseshell cat called Tigger.

PAGE 49
What are reports for?
The following are reports: 2, 3, 5

Planning reports
Football, rugby and netball should be coloured red. Long jump, high jump and relay race should be coloured blue.

Sports added will vary, but should be coloured according to the key.

PAGE 51
Story openings
The unanswered question is:
Who is living in the house?

What happens next?
Answers will vary, but might include:
1   You are peering through the net curtains

during the day, when they suddenly open and a face looks back at you.
2   You creep inside the house and the door slams shut behind you, trapping you inside.

Story endings
Answers will vary, but might include:
You discover that a scientist has bought the house. She has a daughter your age and you become friends.

PAGE 53
Developing characters
Answers will vary, but one mark should be awarded for each character development.

Writing about settings
Answers will vary, but might include:
1   The neighbour squeezed through a gap in the prickly hedge.
2   Moonlight spread across the garden like fingers.
3   Silent trees watched the man as he began to dig.

PAGE 55
What is poetry?
The person who writes a poem is called a poet. Poems use rhythm or rhyme to help show an idea in a powerful way. Poems have fewer words than a story, so each one has to work really hard. Most poems contain creative techniques like alliteration, onomatopoeia and personification. Not all poems have to rhyme, but some do.

Writing list poems
Answers will vary, but might include:
Hot is...
The smiling sun,
Steaming mugs of cocoa,
Red-hot chilli peppers
A piping jacuzzi,
Yummy Indian curry,
Sizzling steaks on a barbecue,
Toasty hot water bottle.

Letts Educational
4 Grosvenor Place, London SW1X 7DL
School enquiries: 015395 64911/65921
Parent & student enquiries: 015395 64913
E-mail: mail@lettsandlonsdale.co.uk

Website: www.letts-educational.com

First published 2008

Editorial and design: 2ibooks [publishing solutions] Cambridge

Author: Alison Head
Book concept and development: Helen Jacobs, Publishing Director
Editorial: Sophie London, Senior Commissioning Editor
            Katy Knight, Editorial Assistant
Illustrators: Andy Roberts and Phillip Burrows
Cover design: Angela English

Letts & Lonsdale make every effort to ensure all paper used in our books is made from wood pulp obtained from sustainable and well-managed forests. Every effort has been made to trace copyright holders and obtain their permission for the use of copyright material. The authors and publishers will gladly receive information enabling them to rectify any error or omission in subsequent editions. All facts are correct at time of going to press.

All our Rights Reserved. No part of the publication may be produced, stored in a retrieval system, or transmitted, in any form or by any means, electronic, mechanical, photocopying, recording or otherwise, without the prior permission of Letts Educational.

British Library Cataloging in Publication Data. A CIP record of this book is available from the British Library.

ISBN 9781843158776

Text, design and illustration © Letts Educational Limited 2008

Printed in Italy

What is an adjective?

Circle the adjectives in these sentences.

1. The Earth is round.

2. The cake was delicious.

3. Dad told us a funny joke.

4. Our teacher was happy because we finished our work.

5. The beautiful ballerina danced across the stage.

5

Choosing adjectives

Think of a better word to replace the red adjective in each sentence. Then write the sentence again, using your adjective.

1. A small spider had spun a web among the grass.

   _____

   _____

2. The bad boy stuck out his tongue.

   _____

   _____

3. I am reading a good book.

   _____

   _____

3

TOTAL MARKS 8

31

Verbs

Verbs are action words

Verbs are words that describe actions. They tell us what a person or thing is doing.

The rabbit is **eating**. Eating is a verb.

The children **played**. Played is a verb.

Using verbs

All sentences must contain a verb which tells us what the person or thing in the sentence is doing.

When you are writing, you have to choose the best verb to describe what the subject is doing.

The boy is **running**. The ball is **bouncing**.

Verb tenses

Verbs don't just tell us what is happening. They can tell us when it happens as well.

Verbs change tense to tell us whether something is happening now, has already happened, or will happen in the future.

I walked to school. (past tense)

I am walking to school. (present tense)

I shall walk to school. (future tense)

Lots of past tense verbs end in **ed**.

Key words — tense   past tense   present tense   future tense

Verbs are action words

Underline the verb in each sentence.

1. The boy kicked the ball.
2. It rained all day.
3. The horse trotted around its field.
4. Our teacher collected the books.
5. The man hobbled down the street.

5

Using verbs

Pick the best verb from the box to complete each sentence.

| swims | ate | helping | takes | planned |

1. The girl _____ the cake.
2. A bus _____ us to school.
3. Our goldfish _____ around its bowl.
4. I love _____ Mum in the kitchen.
5. We _____ a big party for Dad's birthday.

5

Verb tenses

Circle the past tense verbs in these sentences.

1. We all laughed at Philip's joke.
2. The scouts cooked sausages on a campfire.
3. Our hamster climbed up the bars of its cage.
4. My class collected money for charity.
5. I looked for my missing football boot.

 *Don't forget, not all past tense verbs end in ed.*

5

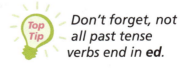

TOTAL MARKS 15

33

Adverbs

How do adverbs work?

Adverbs are words we can use to describe verbs. They help us to say much more about what people or things are doing.

The snowman melted **slowly**.

The man shouted **loudly**.

Using adverbs is a quick and easy way to create a picture in your reader's mind.

Top Tip: Remember, verbs describe actions, e.g. *sing*, *run*, *look*.

Adverbs and verbs

Verbs can tell us *what* a person or thing is doing, but they don't always tell us much about *how*. Adverbs can help you to build up a better picture for your reader by explaining how something is done.

Adverbs can change the meaning of a sentence, so you have to choose them carefully.

The girl walked briskly.   The girl walked slowly.

Key words | adverb

How do adverbs work?

Underline the adverbs in these sentences.

1 The plane climbed steadily.

2 Dad yawned sleepily.

3 The children waved cheerfully.

4 We crossed the road carefully.

5 Eve did her homework neatly.

5

Adverbs and verbs

Pick an adverb from the box to complete each sentence.

| suddenly | quickly | politely | angrily | nervously |

1 The boy shouted _____ at his younger brother.

2 Amy read her story _____ to the class.

3 Connor ran _____ to answer the door.

4 The girls asked _____ for a drink.

5 A bird swooped _____ over the garden.

5

TOTAL MARKS   10

35

Synonyms

What are synonyms?

Synonyms are words with similar meanings.

cold	→	chilly
shoe	→	boot
run	→	jog
quickly	→	rapidly

 *You can find lists of synonyms in a special book called a thesaurus.*

Using synonyms

Synonyms help you to avoid having to use the same word again and again in your writing. This will make it more interesting to read.

My hair was **wet** and my clothes were **wet** through.

My hair was **soaked** and my clothes were **wet** through.

Read your writing carefully and, if you find that you keep using the same word, try to think of a different word you could use instead.

 Key words   synonym   thesaurus

What are synonyms?

Match up the pairs of synonyms.

1 pretty   ocean
2 broken   jacket
3 walk   beautiful
4 coat   saunter
5 light   smashed
6 sea   lamp

6

Using synonyms

Write these sentences again, replacing one of the bold words with a suitable synonym from the box to avoid repetition.

> meadow   rushed   gloomy   broom

1 The **dark** corridor led into a **dark** courtyard.

   _____

2 The cupboard held a dustpan and **brush** and a long-handled **brush**.

   _____

   _____

3 We walked across the **field** to a flowery **field**, where we ate our picnic.

   _____

   _____

4 I **hurried** out of the house and **hurried** to catch the bus.

   _____

4

TOTAL MARKS 10

37

Imagery

Simile

Simile is a creative writing technique where one thing is compared to another using the words *as* or *like*. Similes are great for describing things and creating atmosphere in your stories.

Helen shivered, her face as pale as a ghost.

There are lots of well-known similes, or you can make up your own to use in your writing.

Metaphor

Metaphor is another creative technique that can be used to describe things. With metaphor, a thing is described as if it really were something else.

The moon was a lantern, lighting our way.

Personification

Personification works by describing non-human things using human characteristics.

The flowers danced in the hedgerows.

Flowers do not really dance, but people do. Describing them as if they were dancing people helps the reader to picture how they were moving.

 Top Tip Techniques like simile, metaphor and personification are all types of **imagery**. This means that they help to build up a picture for your reader.

 Key words   simile   metaphor   personification   imagery

38

Simile

Underline the simile in each sentence.

1 Tom gobbled up his pizza like a pig.

2 Katie answered the door as fast as lightning.

3 The laundry fluttered on the line like bunting.

4 The kitten's fur was as soft as silk.

4

Metaphor

Put a tick next to the sentences that contain metaphors.

1 The night was a dark blanket across the landscape. ☐

2 The cake was covered in pink icing, with four white candles. ☐

3 The flower border was a rainbow, stretching down the garden. ☐

4 The sky was deep blue, with fluffy white clouds. ☐

4

Personification

Pick the correct word from each set of brackets, so that each sentence contains personification.

1 The moon (shone / smiled) down on us.

2 The branches of the trees (reached / stuck) out into the darkness.

3 Shadows (crept / moved) across the floor towards us.

4 A strong wind (chased / blew) dry autumn leaves off the trees.

4

TOTAL MARKS   12

Special effects

Alliteration

Thinking about how words sound can help you to write brilliant descriptions.

Start by thinking about the sound at the beginning of words. Grouping words that start with the same sound together can help to draw attention to important bits in your writing. This is called **alliteration**.

Snow White **bit** the **beautiful but bitter** apple.

Onomatopoeia

When you say some words, they sound like the noise they are describing. This is called **onomatopoeia**.

crackle

crunch

pop

screech

 Be careful not to overdo creative techniques. Save them for parts of your writing that you want to draw your reader's attention to.

 Key words   alliteration   onomatopoeia

LEARN

WRITING

40

Alliteration

Pick words from the box to complete each sentence.

> winds   silver   towering   pound   ball

1. Billy bounced a blue _____.

2. Paul paid Peter a _____.

3. Sarah saw _____ stars sparkling.

4. Autumn leaves tumbled from _____ treetops.

5. Whistling _____ whipped wispy clouds.

5

Onomatopoeia

Match up each onomatopoeia with the correct picture.

1.   shatter

2.   drip

3.   bang

4.    fizz

5.    sizzle

5

TOTAL MARKS   10

PRACTISE WRITING

41

Instructions

What are instructions?

Instructions are non-fiction texts that tell you what to do.

There are lots of different types of instructions. Recipes and road signs are types of instructions, as are directions on how to do something. You will also find instructions on packaged foods, medicines and toiletries.

Instructions do not ask you to do something – they tell you how to do it!

> Fix the hinge to part A.
>
> Assemble parts B and C.

This is called the **imperative**. It is just a way of telling someone what to do.

> **Top Tip:** Look in recipe or craft books to see how they use the imperative to tell the reader what to do.

Writing instructions

Instructions are often written as a numbered list, or as bullet points.

The task is broken down into small steps for the reader to follow. You must list them in the correct order or the user will not get the result they need! The steps are often numbered, to make sure that they are carried out in the correct order.

Remember to give your instructions a title too, so your reader knows what the outcome of following them will be.

 Key words   instructions   imperative

What are instructions?

Underline the imperatives in these instructions.

How to make crispy cakes

1 Melt the chocolate over a low heat.

2 Add the crisp rice cereal.

3 Stir until the cereal is coated with the melted chocolate.

4 Spoon the mixture into paper cake cases.

5 Refrigerate until set.

Writing instructions

Number the steps 1–5 to put these instructions into the correct order.

How to wash your hair

Work shampoo into a lather.

Wet hair thoroughly.

Dry hair.

Apply shampoo.

Rinse thoroughly.

 Thinking about how you would actually do a task can help you to put the steps into the correct order.

Persuasive writing

Types of persuasive writing

The aim of **persuasive writing** is to convince the reader to adopt a particular point of view, or to buy a product or visit an attraction.

There are lots of different types of persuasive writing. We are surrounded by it all the time. Adverts on the TV, radio and Internet, and in magazines and newspapers, are all persuasive writing. So are many leaflets and posters.

The language of persuasion

Persuasive writing often contains very few words, so each one is very important. Good writers use lots of powerful adjectives to make whatever they are writing about sound really exciting.

> Hill Heights is *fantastic*. The *most exciting* place to visit this weekend!

Keep your language simple, so that everyone will understand it, especially if you are writing for children. Think about what would persuade you to try the product or attraction yourself. Give reasons why it is a good product or place to visit.

Top Tip: Have a look at adverts, leaflets and posters and think about how they have used language to persuade their readers.

Key words — **persuasive writing**

Types of persuasive writing

Circle the phrases that describe a type of persuasive writing.

a recipe

a postcard

a magazine advert

a road map

a diary

a poster advertising a film

a holiday brochure

a leaflet about a new leisure centre

4

The language of persuasion

Read these sentences about a new film.

a Space Battles is a film with lots of special effects, starring lots of famous actors.

b Space Battles is an exciting film packed with incredible special effects and starring the biggest names in Hollywood.

1 Put a tick in the box beside the sentence you find more persuasive.

2 Underline the powerful adjectives in the sentence you choose.

3 Which sentence has more powerful adjectives?

a   b

3

TOTAL MARKS 7

45

Recounts

What is a recount?

Recounts tell readers about something that has happened.

A recount could be an account of a holiday, a funny story about something that happened to you, or a piece of biographical writing.

> We had a lovely time at the beach yesterday. We built a sandcastle and went in the sea before lunch. After we had eaten we hired a motorboat. In the evening we went out for dinner.
> Sam
>
> Chris Black
> Tall Trees
> Home Town
> UK

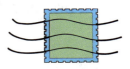

Writing a recount

Recounts are non-fiction writing, so they tend not to include a lot of imagery, like similes, metaphors and personification.

Because they are about an event that has already happened, recounts are written in the past tense. The events are described in the order in which they happened and they are often linked together with **time connectives** like *after that, suddenly* and *all at once*.

> *At first* I did not realise that my bag had gone. *As soon as* I noticed, I went to the lost property office. They took my name and a description of the bag. *By the time* I got home, my bag had been handed in.

Top Tip — *Try using a time line to plan your recount. It will help to ensure you get events in the right order and don't miss anything out.*

Key words: recount   time connective

46

What is a recount?

Write down three different types of recounts.

1. _____

2. _____

3. _____

3

Writing a recount

Underline five time connectives in this recount.

> We went to the animal rescue centre to adopt a pet cat.
>
> First we looked at some kittens and then an old black cat.
>
> After that we saw a lovely tabby with white paws, followed by
>
> a black fluffy cat. Finally we chose a beautiful tortoiseshell
>
> cat called Tigger.

5

TOTAL MARKS 8

47

Reports

What are reports for?

A **report** is an information text about a particular subject. Reports can be about almost any topic, so you will probably have to write them in other classes as well as English.

Reports are organised into topics, rather than chronologically, and they are often written in the present tense.

> The UK buries millions of tons of rubbish in landfill sites each year. Much of this could be recycled.

Planning reports

The information in reports is organised into topics, but that can be harder than it sounds!

Start by researching your topic in books and on the Internet. Decide which bits of information you want to use, then plan it on paper to find a logical way to present the information. Try using a **spidergram** to organise your ideas. It will help you to group your ideas into topics and ensure that you don't miss anything out when you come to write the report.

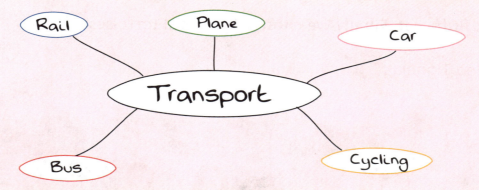

Once you have a spidergram, you can simply write one paragraph for each section of your plan.

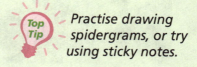

Practise drawing spidergrams, or try using sticky notes.

 Key words   report   spidergram

What are reports for?

Which of these things are reports? Underline your choices.

1 An advert for a new film.

2 Writing about woodland and the animals that live there.

3 A project on the Tudors.

4 A story about a magic lantern.

5 A piece of text about a village in India.

6 A recipe for blueberry muffins.

3

Planning reports

Here is a spidergram for a report about the sports on offer at a school. Colour in the six ideas on this spidergram, so that they match the key. You will get one mark for each.

Key: red = ball games   blue = athletics

Add one more idea for each topic and colour it to match the others, for two further marks.

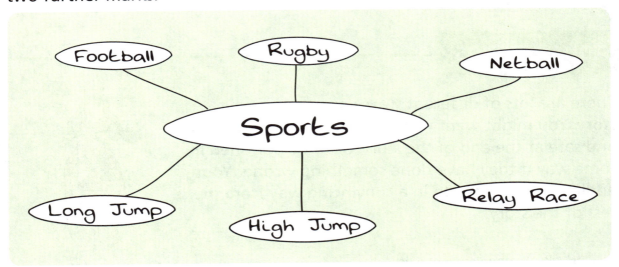

Using colours is a great way to sort your ideas into topics.

8

TOTAL MARKS 11

49

Planning stories

Story openings

Writing stories can be daunting, but you can make it much easier if you spend time planning the story before you start. You need to decide how it will start, what will happen in the middle and how it will end.

A story opening is your first chance to hook your reader. Try to start the action straight away and leave a question unanswered in the first few sentences. That way, the reader has to keep reading to find out what happens next.

Get off to a great start by using lots of strong descriptive words in your opening.

What happens next?

You need to think carefully about what happens to your characters in the story. It is a good idea if they have to face some sort of problem or difficulty. Then you can write about how they overcome it.

Make sure you keep the action going in the middle of the story. It is very easy to start long, rambling descriptions that don't actually keep the plot moving along.

Story endings

There are lots of different ways you can end your story. You might want your characters to be happy and safe at the end of the story, or to be punished in some way if they have done something wrong. Your ending must follow on in a convincing way from the rest of the story.

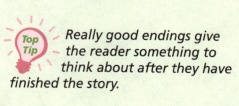

Really good endings give the reader something to think about after they have finished the story.

Story openings

Read this story. It leaves a question unanswered.

> The house on Sycamore Lane had been empty for years. Now there was movement once more behind the grimy net curtains and smoke curling out of the chimney. Strange, purplish smoke. Nobody seemed to know who had moved in.

Tick the unanswered question.

Is the house on fire? ☐   Who is living in the house? ☐

Why doesn't anyone know who has moved in? ☐

1

What happens next?

Reread the story opening above. Imagine you are a character living in the house next door and you decide to find out who is living in the house. Write down two ideas for problems or difficulties you might face in your quest to find out about your new neighbours.

1 _____

_____

2 _____

_____

2

Story endings

Choose your favourite plot idea from the previous section, then think about how your story could end. Write a sentence to say what would happen.

_____

_____

1

PRACTISE

WRITING

TOTAL MARKS 4

51

Characters and settings

Developing characters

Characters are the people in your stories. They are the most important part of a story, because readers don't want to read about boring characters.

Don't try to cram too many characters into your stories. It is better to have two or three that you can describe really well and bring them to life.

Think carefully about what each character is like before you start writing. Don't just imagine what they look like. Think about how they behave and what they say too.

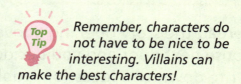

Remember, characters do not have to be nice to be interesting. Villains can make the best characters!

Writing about settings

The setting is the place where the story happens. Describing the setting can be a brilliant way to create the right atmosphere in your story. For example, a science fiction story could have a space-age setting and a ghost story could be set in a haunted house.

Using imagery like simile, metaphor and personification will help you to create really convincing settings.

> The old house crouched in the moonlight, like a troll.

Developing characters

Imagine you are writing a story about a boy who finds some valuable Roman treasure in his garden. The boy's mean neighbour decides to dig up the boy's garden at night to try to find some more. Choose either the boy or the neighbour, then write a character profile.

1 Name: _____

2 Age: _____

3 Personality:

☐ greedy ☐ brave

☐ honest ☐ dishonest

4 Appearance: _____

5 How does he feel about the treasure? _____

6 Descriptive word or phrase to describe how he moves:

_____

Top Tip *Having two characters that are complete opposites can work really well. Think about the story of Beauty and the Beast!*

6

Writing about settings

The neighbour is about to dig up the boy's garden in the middle of the night. Think of powerful words or phrases to complete these sentences about the garden setting.

1 The neighbour squeezed through a gap in the _____ hedge.

2 Moonlight spread across the garden like _____.

3 Silent trees _____ the man as he began to dig.

3

TOTAL MARKS 9

Poetry

What is poetry?

A lot of people find poetry scary, but there is no need to. It can be great fun!

A poem is a type of text that uses rhythm or **rhyme** to show an idea in a vivid way, along with powerful vocabulary. Lots of poems have rhyming words at the end of each line, but they don't have to.

Most poems contain far fewer words than you would find in a story, so every word has to work really hard. Poets often use alliteration, onomatopoeia and personification to add to the effect.

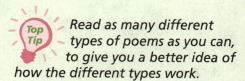

Top Tip: Read as many different types of poems as you can, to give you a better idea of how the different types work.

Writing list poems

Writing poetry doesn't need to be difficult! A **list poem** is simply a list of powerful descriptions, based on the same subject. The descriptions in the list don't need to rhyme and each one is self-contained, so you can use a different creative technique for each one if you want to.

Sweet is…

jolly jellies, jiving, — alliteration / personification

crunchy crispy cakes, — alliteration and onomatopoeia

ripe cherries, like jewels, — simile

pink candy floss clouds. — metaphor

Key words: rhyme, list poem

54

What is poetry?

Pick words from the box to complete this piece of writing about poetry.

rhyme   words   personification   rhythm   poet

The person who writes a poem is called a _____.

Poems use _____ or rhyme to help show an idea in a powerful way. Poems have fewer _____ than a story, so each one has to work really hard. Most poems contain creative techniques like alliteration, onomatopoeia and _____.

Not all poems have to _____, but some do.

5

Writing list poems

Add five lines to complete this list poem.

Hot is…

The smiling sun,

Steaming mugs of cocoa,

_____

_____

_____

_____

_____

5

TOTAL MARKS 10

Glossary

adjective a word or phrase that describes a noun

adverb a word or phrase that describes a verb

alliteration a phrase where most or all of the words begin with the same sound

apostrophe a punctuation mark used for contraction when two words are joined, e.g. he'll, or to show possession, e.g. We'll collect Dad's car.

author the person who writes a text

autobiography the story of someone's life that they write themselves

biography the story of someone's life written by someone else

blurb information on the back of a book designed to give the reader an idea of what it is about

character the people or animals that a story is about

clause a distinct part of a sentence including a verb

comma a punctuation mark that shows when to pause, separates clauses or separates items in a list

common noun a noun that names ordinary things, e.g. book, car

comprehension understanding what a text is about

contraction when words are shortened, or two words are joined, by removing letters and replacing with an apostrophe, e.g. can't, won't

curriculum vitae a summary of a person's experience and qualifications

dialogue a spoken or written conversation between two people

direct speech words that are actually spoken, enclosed in speech marks

exclamation mark a punctuation mark that can be used instead of a full stop to indicate surprise or that an order has been made, e.g. Ouch!

fact a piece of information that can be tested and proven to be true

fiction stories with imaginary characters, settings or events

future tense describes things that will happen in the future

glossary a collection of useful words and their meanings

imagery words used to build up a picture in a story, including simile, metaphor and personification

imperative a way of using verbs to give an order or instruction, e.g. Turn left at the traffic lights.

index an alphabetical list of the topics in a book

instructions texts that tell people what to do, or how to do something, e.g. recipes

ISBN a unique number on the back of a book used by booksellers and libraries

list poem a poem that consists of a list of descriptions based on a single theme

metaphor where a writer describes something as if it were something else, e.g. The bird was an arrow, tearing across the sky.

narrator the person from whose viewpoint a story is told, who may or may not be a character in the story

non-fiction writing that is not fictional, including information texts about real people and places, letters, instructions and reports

noun a word that names a thing or feeling

onomatopoeia where a word sounds like the noise it describes, e.g. crash, shatter

past tense describes things that have already happened

personification a writing technique in which human characteristics are used to describe non-human things, e.g. Shadows crept across the floor.

persuasive writing writing that aims to persuade the reader to adopt a particular viewpoint, or buy a product or service, e.g. magazine adverts, posters, leaflets

plural more than one of something, usually made by adding s or es, e.g. dogs, dresses

possessive apostrophe an apostrophe used to show that something belongs to someone, e.g. Sarah's homework

present tense describes things that are happening now

pronoun a word used instead of a noun to avoid having to use the same noun again, e.g. I, she, we, me

proper noun a noun that names a specific person, thing or place, e.g. Chris, Manchester, Friday

punctuation marks used to make writing clear, e.g. .,!?"

question mark a punctuation mark used in place of a full stop to show that a question is being asked

recount a report that describes events in chronological order or the order in which they happened

report an information text about a particular subject

reported speech speech reported in a text, but not directly quoted, e.g. She said she was tired.

rhyme an effect created when endings of a pair or group of words sound the same, e.g. rabbit, habit

scanning reading quickly to find a specific piece of information

sentence a unit of text that makes sense on its own

simile where a writer compares one thing with another, using the words as or like, e.g. as bold as brass

simple sentence a sentence containing one clause

singular one of something, e.g. a bird

skimming reading quickly to understand the main meaning of a piece of text

speaking and listening the skill of being able to listen to ideas and comment on them

speech marks punctuation marks that surround direct speech. Other punctuation goes inside them, e.g. "Goodbye," said Mum.

spidergram a diagram that can help writers to organise their ideas before writing reports and recounts

subject the person or thing in a sentence that carries out the action, e.g. Amy bit the apple.

synonym a word with exactly or nearly the same meaning as another word, e.g. hot, warm

tense tells us when something is happening

thesaurus a book of synonyms

time connective a word or phrase that connects different parts of a text to show when things happened

verb a doing or being word, e.g. walk, sleep

Notes

NOTES

NOTES